Chris Powling

Pirates

Illustrated by Chris Mould

This book belongs to

OXFORD
UNIVERSITY PRESS

Great Clarendon Street, Oxford OX2 6DP

Oxford University Press is a department of the University of Oxford.
It furthers the University's objective of excellence in research, scholarship,
and education by publishing worldwide in

Oxford New York

Auckland Bangkok Buenos Aires Cape Town Chennai
Dar es Salaam Delhi Hong Kong Istanbul Karachi Kolkata
Kuala Lumpur Madrid Melbourne Mexico City Mumbai Nairobi
São Paulo Shanghai Taipei Tokyo Toronto

Oxford is a registered trade mark of Oxford University Press
in the UK and in certain other countries

First published 2003

Paperback ISBN 0–19–910843–9

3 5 7 9 10 8 6 4 2

Printed in Spain

Contents

Pirate power

I like the sound of pirates.
Don't you?

In my head, I hear
the *SWISH* of a pirate cutlass…
the **BOOM** of a pirate cannon…
and the CLINK of pirate gold
in a treasure chest. These make
me think of the olden days.

I like the look of pirates, too.
Don't you?

I like their wild, wind-swept hair. I like their loose, sea-salty clothes. I like their earrings and eyepatches and the parrots that perch on their shoulders. These also remind me of the olden days.

Pirate Plunder

Doubloons were Spanish gold coins. Pesos, called 'pieces of eight', were made of silver. Both, along with other treasure, came from mines in South America. They were then transported to Europe by huge fleets of ships. This gave pirates their chance. Soon any cargo became fair game – especially when carried by leading traders like The East India Company. Remember, pirates also had to steal rope, sails, spars and other sea supplies (including ships and sailors) to stay afloat.

Pretend pirates and real pirates

Actually, I quite fancy being a pirate. Don't you?

In the olden days, pirates were cool. I know this from the pirate stories I've read. I'd love to be Captain Hook in the story of **PETER PAN.** I'd love to be Long John Silver in the story of **TREASURE ISLAND.** And I'd love to be almost anyone in the stories of **CAPTAIN PUGWASH.**

⬅ Captain Hook — enemy of Peter Pan.

Pirate Talk

Like all sailors, pirates used lots of words and phrases to do with the sea, ships and sailing. In books, this talk tends to be made even more piratical. 'Shiver me timbers', for instance, means 'I'm amazed!' and 'smart as paint' says 'I like the look of it'. If something is simple and pleasing then it's 'neat as kiss me hand'. Maybe you can discover, or invent, some pirate talk for yourself.

Hold on, though....

All these are make-believe pirates, aren't they? And they belong in make-believe stories. What about pirates in real life? Were they really just like this – even in the olden days?

We'd better check out some of the facts.
Here's a list of what pirates used to wear:

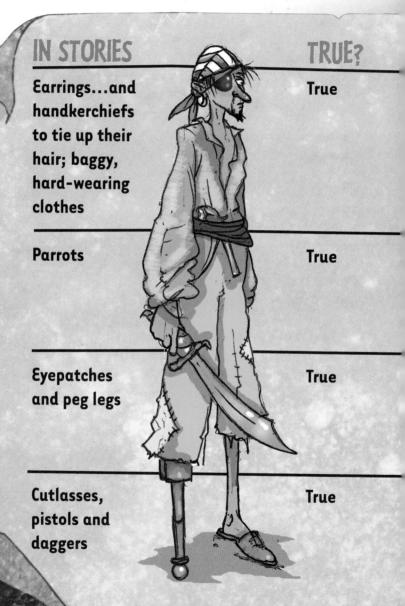

IN STORIES	TRUE?
Earrings...and handkerchiefs to tie up their hair; baggy, hard-wearing clothes	True
Parrots	True
Eyepatches and peg legs	True
Cutlasses, pistols and daggers	True

IN REAL LIFE

It was hard work sailing a ship. So clothes had to be tough, comfy and cheap. Only pirate captains could afford to be flashy.

Pirates loved keeping pets aboard ship — and parrots were much less trouble than monkeys.

Sailing a ship was very risky — especially a fighting ship. Like other sailors in the olden days, pirates often got badly hurt.

Pirates wore plenty of weapons to make themselves scary. That way they might win without a fight. If not, then they needed all the weapons they could carry.

Pirates at sea

So far, then, the storybooks get it right. Are they right about pirate ships as well?

Mostly they are, yes. Pirate ships tended to be small and swift – just like *The Jolly Roger* in **PETER PAN**, the *Hispaniola* in **TREASURE ISLAND** and *The Black Pig* in **CAPTAIN PUGWASH**. Pirates needed to make a fast getaway so speed was much more important than size. Of course, their ships always bristled with guns to terrify their victims. But very few pirate ships were as big as a man o' war in the Royal Navy.

So far so good, then.

➲ The ideal pirate ship was small, swift and scary.

Here, though, are some facts that don't quite fit:

IN STORIES	TRUE?
The flag of a pirate ship is always the 'Jolly Roger' – a skull and crossbones. 	Not true
Pirate flags are always black and white	Not true
 Pirates always obey their captain	Not true
Pirates attack by firing their guns sideways on – what's called a 'broadside'. 	Not true
Pirates are fair fighters	Not true

IN REAL LIFE

Some pirate flags showed
a whole skeleton...or a
bleeding heart, a spear,
a cutlass or some other scary sign.

Often they were red — meaning "we will
shed your blood without mercy."

They did as they were told in battle or
when sailing the ship. At other times they
took a vote about what they should do.
They could even vote for a new captain!

Pirates preferred to sneak up at the back,
or 'stern' of a ship in rowing boats. This
meant the ships they won were undamaged.

Usually they out-numbered and
out-gunned their victims.

Oh dear....

The truth about pirates

Only some pirate stories stay true-to-life, it seems. Others play around with the facts.

For instance, those maps that guide you to buried treasure are a lovely idea… but most pirates had no treasure to bury. They lost it in gambling and wild parties. Also, only once – in 1829 – was someone forced to 'walk the plank'.

Pirate Hunting Grounds

Most European pirates sailed in the Caribbean (sometimes called 'The Spanish Main'). These were known as 'buccaneers'. Others, named 'corsairs', preferred the Mediterranean Sea and the Indian Ocean. Pirates hid themselves anywhere that was safe and secret. Their most famous base was the island of Tortuga near Haiti.

In real life, pirates simply threw their enemies overboard. Or they left them on a lonely island – a punishment called 'marooning'.

← One more step and...SPLASH!

Stories can miss fascinating facts as well. Why are there not more tales about women pirates, I wonder – such as Anne Bonny and Mary Read?

And what about Grace O'Malley, the Irish pirate? Or Mrs Cheng, in the South China Sea, who commanded hundreds of ships? All these were real-life pirates. Yet, in stories, it's men who have all the....

Fun?

Mrs Cheng was as scary as any man.

No, that isn't right either.

In the olden days, going to sea wasn't much fun for men or women. Mostly, it was smelly, nasty and dangerous.

Ordinary sailors often became pirates for a fairer share of food and money. Also, there were more of them to sail the ship. Life would be easier, they thought.

But they were wrong.

Catching pirates

Life as a pirate could be even harder.
The safest way to succeed was to be
a 'privateer' like Sir Henry Morgan
or Sir Francis Drake. A privateer was
given a sort of 'pirate permit' by the
government to attack foreign ships.
Without this to protect
you, you were bound
to be caught sooner
or later.

Punishing the Pirates

By the year 1720, more than fifteen pirate ships were sailing in the Caribbean alone. Each carried about eighty pirates and at least twenty guns. No wonder governments took action. They made new laws, offered huge rewards and sent warships to hunt them down. By 1725, it's reckoned, most pirates had been caught. Already the world was too small for them to find a safe hiding place.

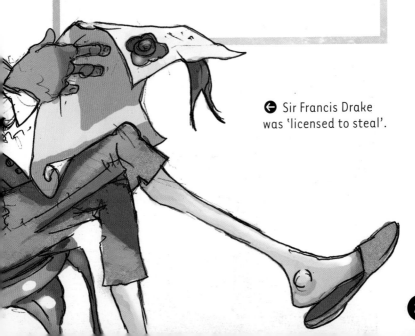

⬅ Sir Francis Drake was 'licensed to steal'.

When you were, you faced a horrible death. Can you imagine being cut to pieces on the deck of your own ship? This is what happened to Edward Teach – known as 'Blackbeard'. Bartholomew Roberts, nicknamed 'Black Bart' died in much the same way.

◗ The end of Blackbeard... or maybe Black Bart.

As for Captain Kidd, he was hung in chains at Execution Dock. Such was the fate of thieves, bullies and murderers in the olden days.

Remember, that's all pirates were – simply thieves, bullies and murderers.

Today's pirates

And that's what pirates still are today.

Oh yes… they haven't disappeared altogether. Sometimes we hear about them in news reports. Using powerful speedboats, they launch attacks on giant container ships. These are easier to rob than you think because they can be crewed by only half a dozen people.

So where are the stories about modern pirates?

Probably, they're not written yet. We may have to wait for these until our days become the olden days. That's when authors can play around with real life as much as they like – spinning wonderful, make-believe yarns about adventure and bravery and freedom.

For we mustn't let facts cramp our dreams.
In a story we can live any life we choose.

That's why, even now, I love the sound
of pirates in my head:

the *SWISH* of a pirate cutlass...
the **BOOM** of a pirate cannon...
and the CLINK of pirate gold in a
treasure chest.

So I still fancy being a pirate
– in a book, that is.

Don't you?

Glossary

 cargo
Cargo is things that are loaded on to a ship to be delivered somewhere else.　　**7**

 cannon
A cannon is a gun that is too big for someone to carry. It fires heavy metal balls.　　**4, 29**

 cutlass
A cutlass is a short, curved sword for hacking.　　**4, 10, 29**

 dagger
A dagger is a very short sword with two sharp edges.　　**10**

 gambling
Gambling is making bets for money.　　**16**

pistol

A pistol is a small gun which is held in the hand. **10**

plunder

Plunder is another name for stolen property. **7**

privateer

A privateer is a pirate who works for the government. **22**

skeleton

A skeleton is all the bones inside the body. **15**

weapon

A weapon is something used to hurt another person in a fight, such as a gun or knife. **11**

Reading Together

Oxford Reds have been written by leading children's authors who have a passion for particular non-fiction subjects. So as well as up-to-date information, fascinating facts and stunning pictures, these books provide powerful writing which draws the reader into the text.

Oxford Reds are written in simple language, checked by educational advisors. There is plenty of repetition of words and phrases, and all technical words are explained. They are an ideal vehicle for helping your child develop a love of reading – by building fluency, confidence and enjoyment.

You can help your child by reading the first few pages out loud, then encourage him or her to continue alone. You could share the reading by taking turns to read a page or two. Or you could read the whole book aloud, so your child knows it well before tackling it alone.

Oxford Reds will help your child develop a love of reading and a lasting curiosity about the world we live in.

Sue Palmer
Writer and Literacy Consultant